EARLY ELEMENTARY

BLACK KEY BLAST!

Six Pre-Staff Solos
with Accompaniment

by Wendy Stevens

ISBN 978-1-4803-6046-4

WILLIS MUSIC

EXCLUSIVELY DISTRIBUTED BY

HAL•LEONARD®
CORPORATION

7777 W. BLUEMOUND RD. P.O. BOX 13819 MILWAUKEE, WI 53213

Visit Hal Leonard Online at
www.halleonard.com

2

Movin' and Groovin'

Words and Music by
Wendy Stevens

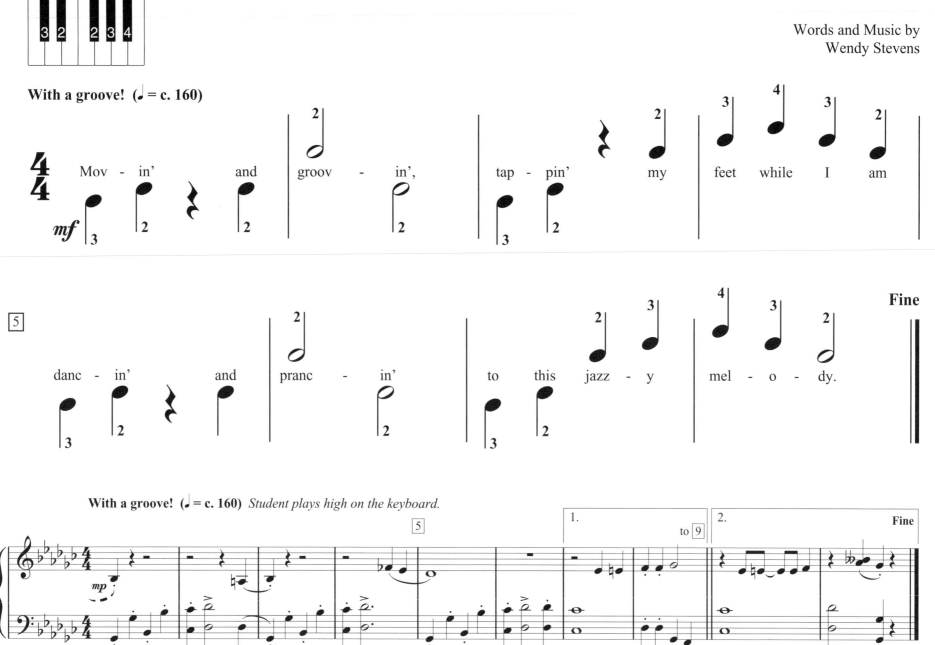

With a groove! (♩ = c. 160)

Mov - in' and groov - in', tap - pin' my feet while I am

danc - in' and pranc - in' to this jazz - y mel - o - dy. **Fine**

With a groove! (♩ = c. 160) *Student plays high on the keyboard.*

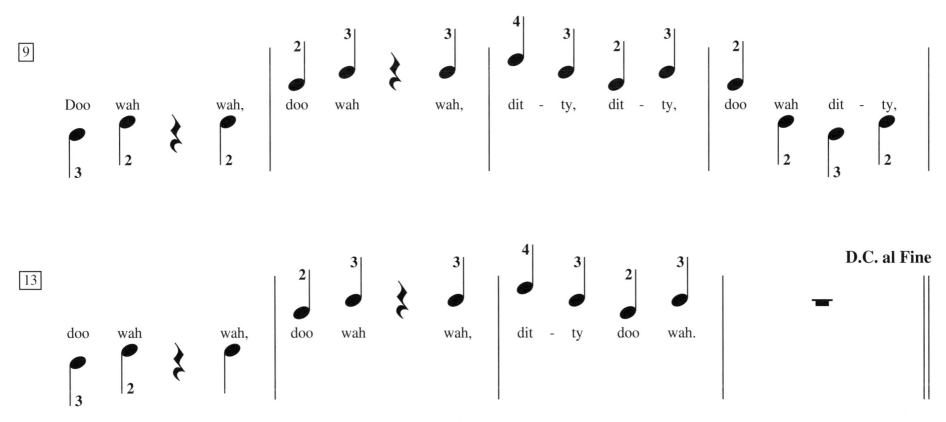

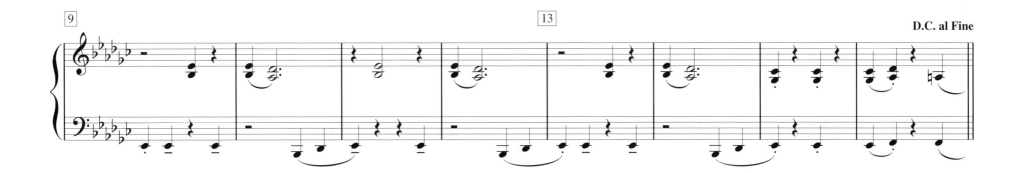

Click Clock Click

Words and Music by
Wendy Stevens

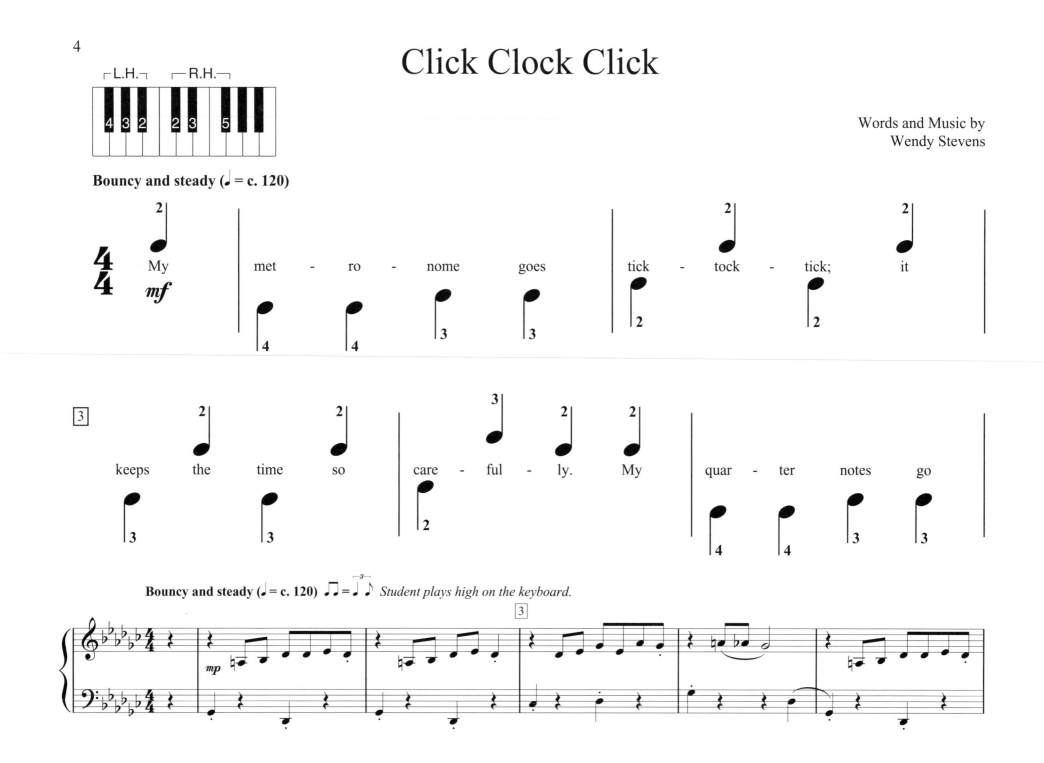

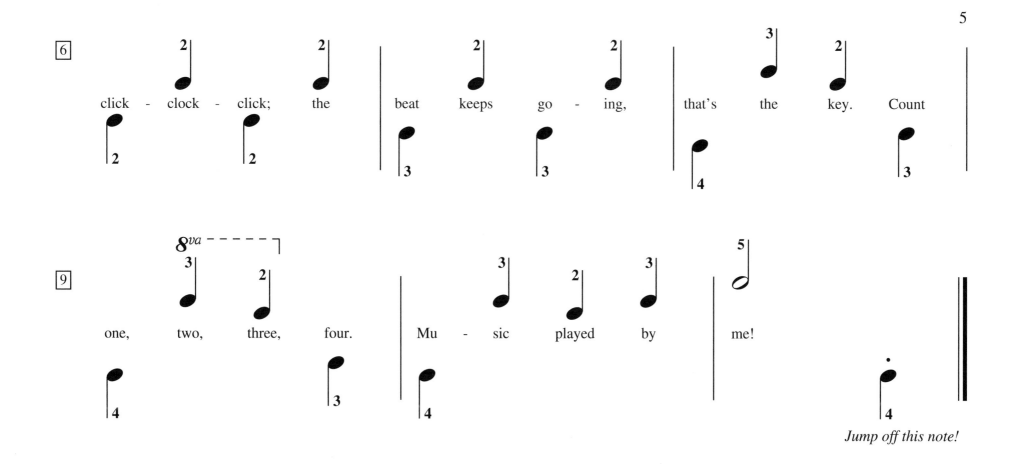

My Imaginary Friend

Words and Music by
Wendy Stevens

Hop off this note!

Round in Circles

Words and Music by
Wendy Stevens

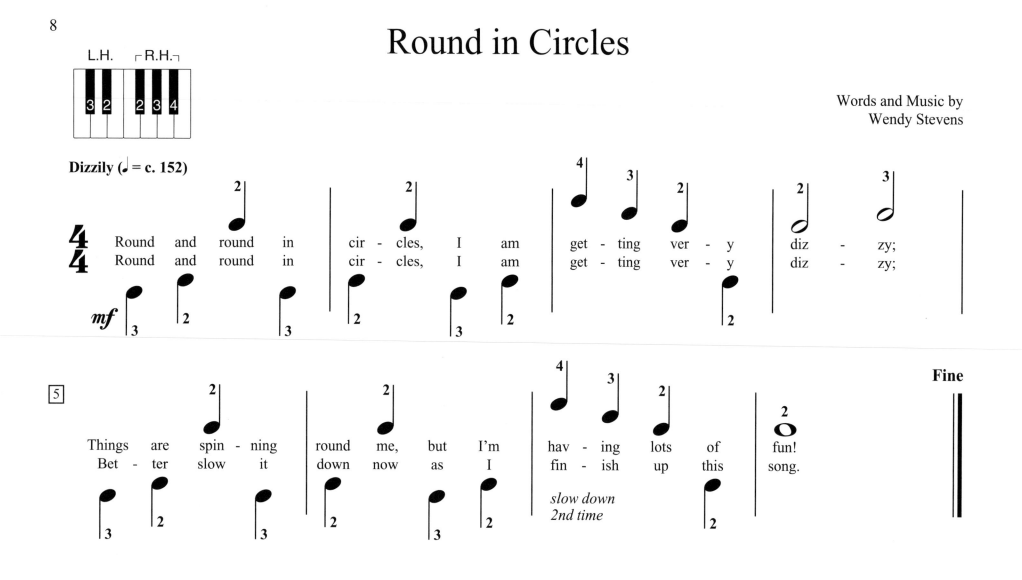

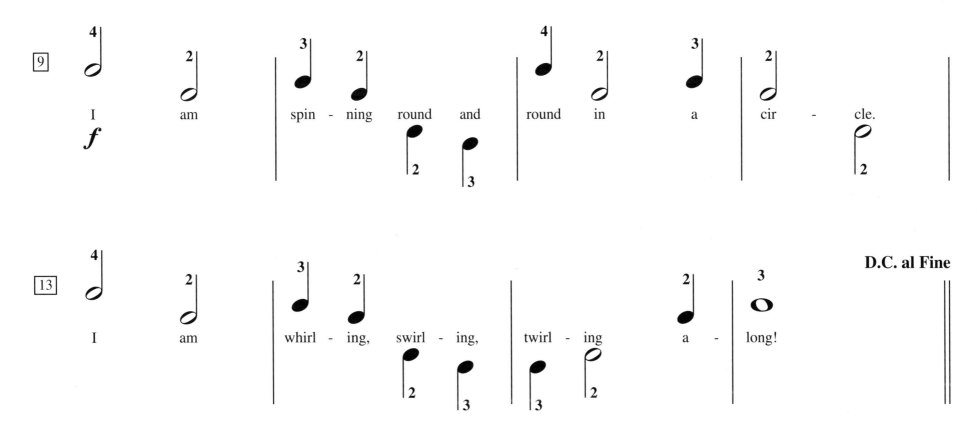

I Am the Princess

Words and Music by
Wendy Stevens

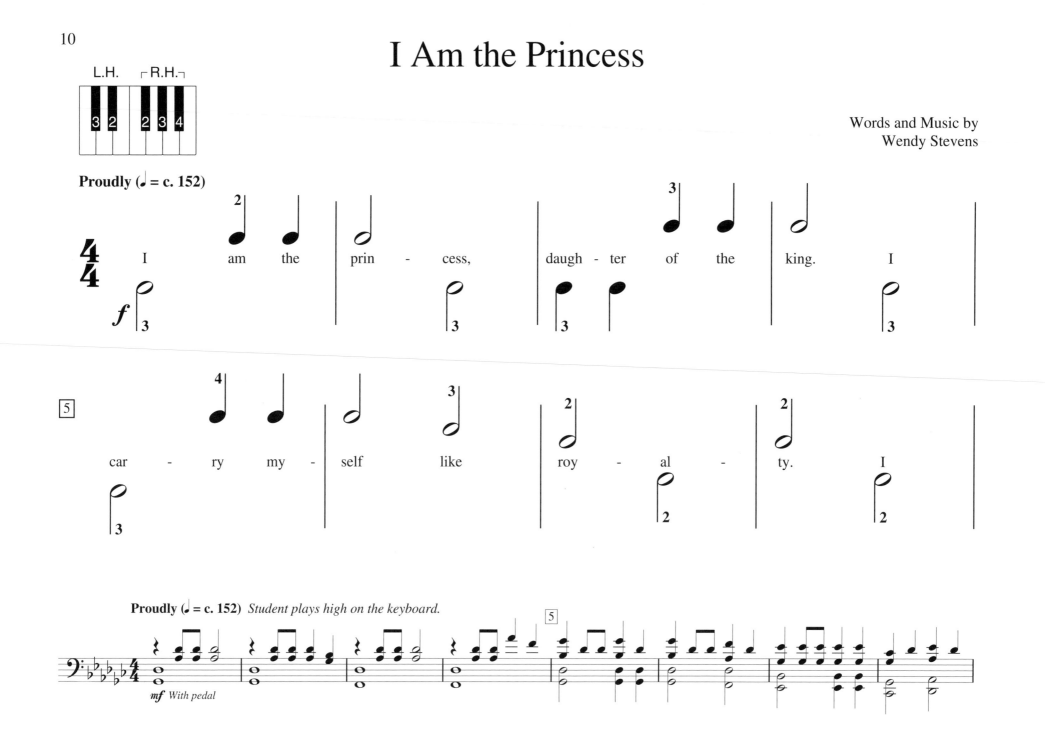

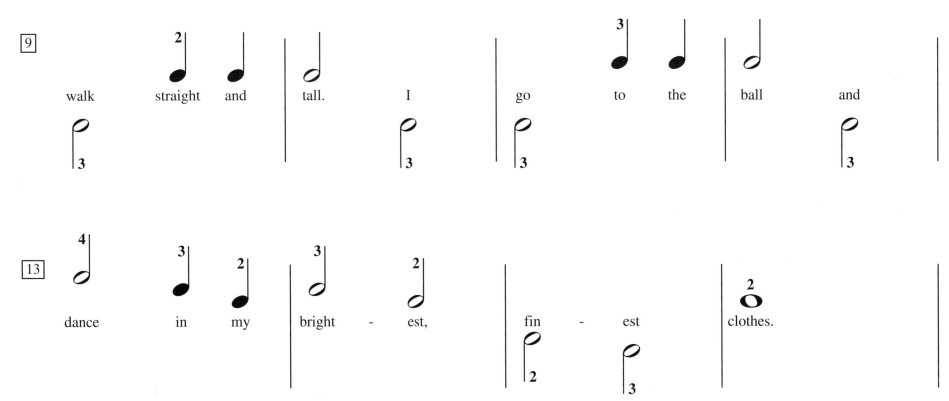

12

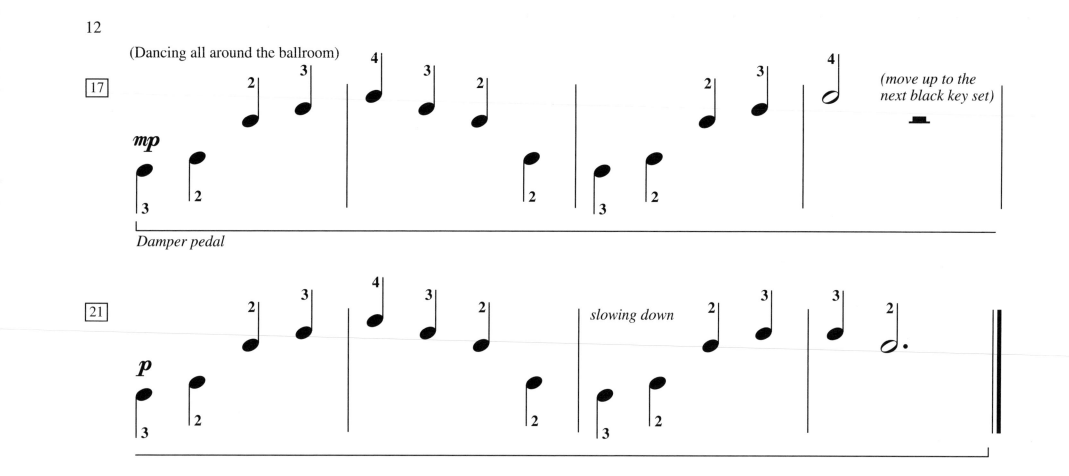

Ninja Power

Words and Music by
Wendy Stevens

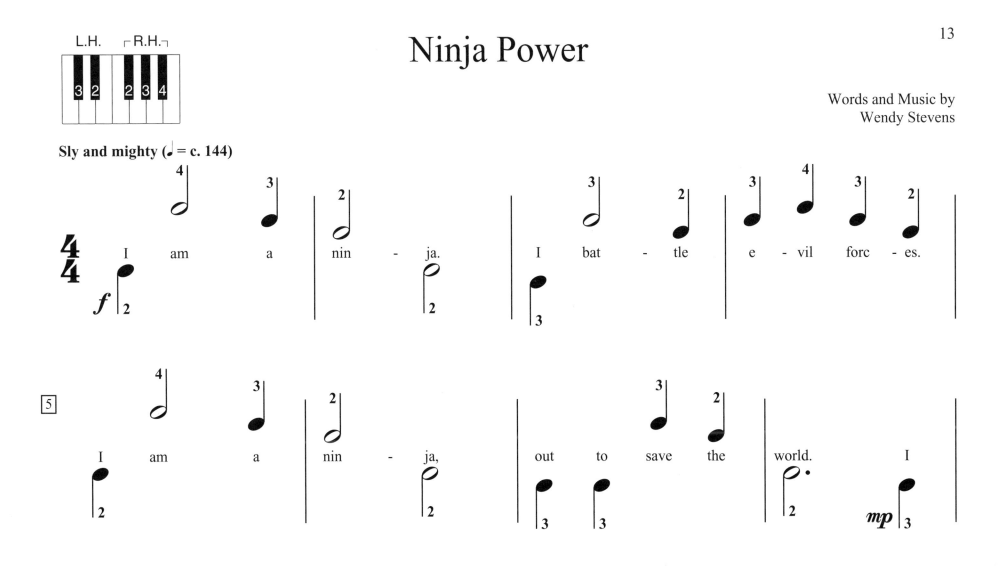

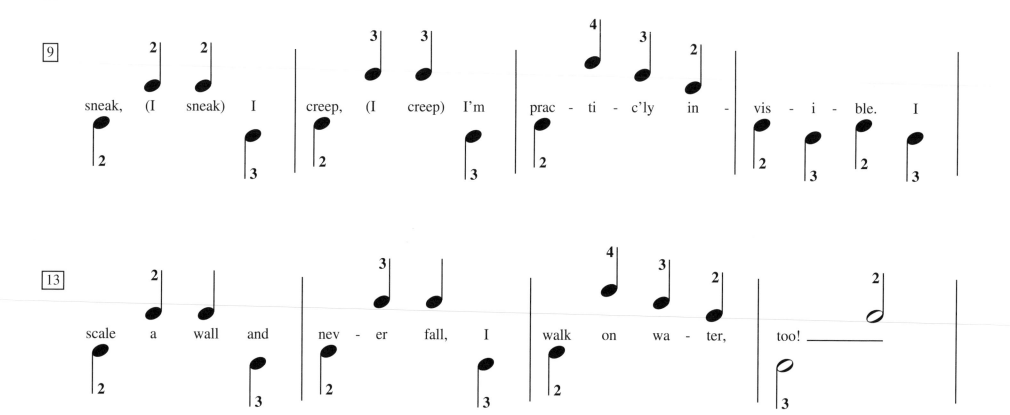

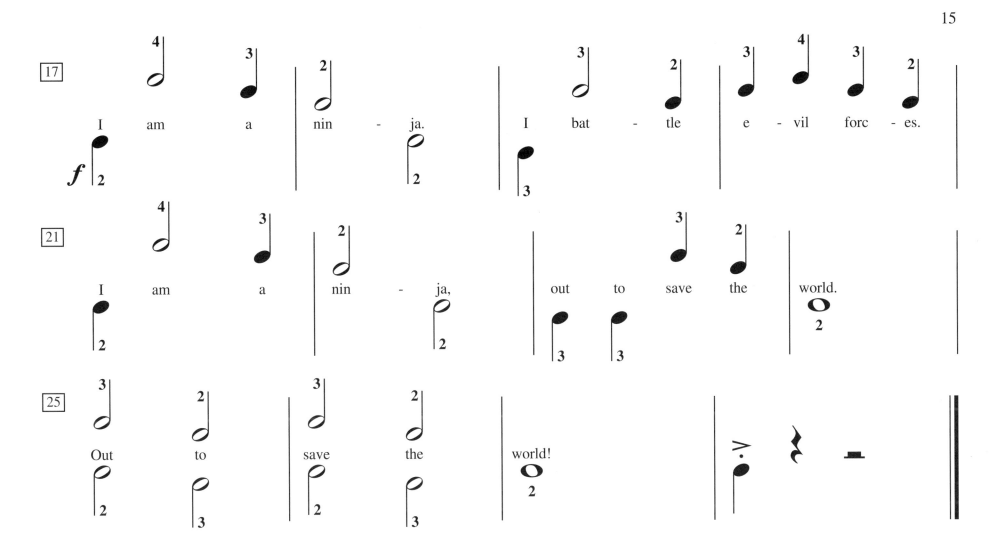

Wendy Stevens is a composer, pianist, teacher, and clinician. She received her Bachelor of Music in Piano Pedagogy and her Masters of Music in Theory and Composition from Wichita State University where she graduated *summa cum laude*. Wendy has been a recipient of the MTNA stAR award (Student Achievement Recognition Award). She has also taught theory at Wichita State University and adjudicates for music events in her area. In addition to her studio teaching, she has served as a church musician playing the piano for more than 20 years.

Wendy is a member of MTNA, KMTA, and her local association WMMTA. She has served as president of WMMTA and has also served on the board for KMTA. She is a nationally certified teacher of music and a member of ASCAP (American Society of Composers, Authors and Publishers).

Wendy enjoys composing and presenting workshops on creativity, composition, business practices, and technology. She maintains a popular blog for piano teachers at **www.ComposeCreate.com**.